Mama Says

Mama Says

The Best Advice from Some of the World's Best Mothers

Alicia Alvrez

CONARI PRESS

First published in 2004 by Conari Press,
an imprint of Red Wheel/Weiser, LLC
York Beach, ME

With offices at:
368 Congress Street
Boston, MA 02210
www.redwheelweiser.com

Library of Congress Cataloging-in-Publication Data
Mama says : the best advice from some of the world's best mothers /
[compiled by] Alicia Alvrez.
        p. cm.
  ISBN 1-57324-870-3 (alk. paper)
  1. Conduct of life—Quotations, maxims, etc. 2. Mothers—
Quotations. I. Alvrez, Alicia.
  PN6084.C556M25 2004
  158.1—dc22   2003024717

Typeset in Dom Casual and Brush Script by Maxine Ressler
Printed in Canada
TCP

11   10   09   08   07   06   05   04
      8   7   6   5   4   3   2   1

The paper used in this publication meets the minimum requirements of
the American National Standard for Information Sciences—Permanence
of Paper for Printed Library Materials Z39.48-1992 (R1997).

For the women who raised us

Contents

Acknowledgments

Many thanks to all the men and women who contributed to this collection, those who sent in their mothers' sayings and those mothers who contributed what they say to their kids.

A bouquet of gratitude to Annette Madden, who made this book possible by doing a great deal of the collecting, and who was instrumental in the creation of this idea in the first place.

Thanks to Jan Johnson for believing in this book, and to all the folks at Red Wheel/Weiser, who make the fact that others are reading it possible.

Mothers Do Say

Sooner or later we all quote our mothers.

— Bern Williams

Amen, Bern. I don't even know who Bern is, but I came across the quote while putting this book together. It seems to sum up all that I want to say about the origins of this book.

I had been going along my merry way, writing women's trivia, when my friend Annette said, apropos of something, "Well, as my mother always says, 'God don't like ugly.'" Huh, I wondered, what does *that* mean? Then, as I pondered further, I thought, how wise.

It got me thinking of all that we hear at our mothers' knees and how much we remember even decades later—how much their words have impacted us and how often we end up with their exact words coming out of our mouths, attributed or not. "Wouldn't it make a great book to collect these sayings?" I asked Annette.

What *are* the things our mothers told us that we remember forever? With Annette's help, that's the question I posed to friends, acquaintances, friends of friends, and strangers. The answers poured in from around the world. Those who wanted to be named were. Those who wished to remain anonymous are.

The advice came in all kinds: funny, touching, useful, trivial, mean, silly, and profound. In many cases, it's not the message so much as the way it is said that is so memorable. Many times, it's clear that it is inherited wisdom, received from their mothers who learned it from theirs and back into the untraceable past. In this way, these sayings represent a lineage of mothers' wisdom—not always kind, not always useful, but always true to the intention of teaching the young ones in their care how to survive in the world.

It's my hope that, taken all together, this collection will bring many smiles and even a few out-and-out laughs of identification or recognition. You might even learn a thing or two.

We mothers have a lot to say. Hey, you kids out there: Are you paying attention?

1

The Proper Comportment of a Lady

Times may pass, standards may change, but throughout history, moms have always had very strong ideas about how their daughters should behave themselves—and they will always make sure we hear about it!

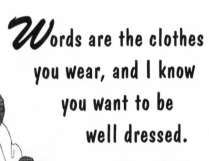

*W*ords are the clothes
you wear, and I know
you want to be
well dressed.

—*Naomi Judd's
mother*

*A*lways wear white gloves
when traveling to Boston.

—*My mother*

*N*ever say "bucket;" say "pail." Never say "cellar;" say "utility room."

—*A friend's mother*

*N*ever wear plaids with stripes.

—*Ruth Segall, Judith Segall's mother*

S it properly . . . the world
isn't interested in the color
of your pants.

—*A mother in* Grace Notes

I don't care how small the top on that two-piece bathing suit is. You just make sure the bottom covers your bellybutton, because I feel something here that it is *obscene* to show your bellybutton!

—*Dotty Cala's mother, while beating a clenched fist against her breast in a much-used Italian-Catholic gesture*

12

*L*ooking good is
feeling good.

—*Cynthia Cotton,*
mother of Blythe Cotton

*N*ever go out of
the house without
your lipstick on.

—*Susan Tumminia, Tyler's mother in*
Real Simple *magazine*

13

Keep your nose clean.

—*Stephanie LaPierre's mom*

Sit still. You're as jumpy as
a cat before a storm.

—*A friend's mother*

*B*rush your kitchen
[meaning the hair at the nape
of your neck if it curled up].

—*Odette Clayton Charbonnet, Joyce
Charbonnet Hayward's mother*

W e don't do that (or wear that, speak like that, make those kinds of faces, listen to that kind of music, etc.). Remember who you are!

—*Marcella Conley's mother*

*C*ross your legs at the ankle, not the knee.

—*My mother*

Ladies never poop!

—*Anne Hollingworth's mother*

"Hey" is for horses, not for people.

—*Patricia Ashton's mother*

*G*o change your dress.

—*A friend's mother, after Sunday school*

*P*ut on a little lipstick so you don't look pale.

—*Cynthia Cotton, mother of Blythe Cotton*

19

*E*veryone has to slip off
their shoulder pads sometimes.

—*Mother, in* Mapping the Edge

*N*ice boys do not ask
girls unfair questions.

—*A friend's mother*

Smiling is a gift of intimacy. . . . Nice young ladies [give] such tender responses only to their husbands.

—*Mother, in* In the Name of Salome

*G*et your nose out of
that book and say
hello to our
company.

—*My mother*

*H*old your stomach in when
you're young. Then it will be
habit when you get older.

—*A friend's mom*

*W*alk like a lady,
with small steps—you walk
like a truck driver.

—*Stephanie LaPierre's mom*

*N*ever hang around on park benches. People will think you're a cheap girl.

—*Anne Hollingworth's mother*

You know, dear, birds of a
feather flock together.

—*Robin Mastro's mother*

You are known by the
company you keep.

—*A friend's mother*

Pretty is as pretty does!

—*Sheri Short's mother*

Don't whistle.
It's not ladylike.

—*Barb Parmet's mother*

*N*o pins in your slip strap!
You might be in an accident.

—*A friend's mother*

*A*lways send a thank you
note for a present, and always
bring a hostess gift if you are
invited to someone's house.

—*My mother*

*K*eep your voice down.
Nobody wants to know
your business.

—*A friend's mother*

*K*eep a curb on your tongue.

—*English mothers*

Don't scrape the bottom
of the barrel.

—*Robin Mastro's mother,
on her improper friends*

Don't be going out looking
like a Fiji islander.

—*A friend's mother, when her mother
thought her hair was a mess*

29

*G*et that hair out of your
eyes, young lady.

—*My mother*

*D*on't say you're sweaty;
ladies don't sweat, they glow.

—*Lori Pottinger's mother*

30

Keep your elbows off the table; that's bad manners. Don't slurp your soup or eat with your fingers. Put your hand over your mouth when you cough. Say "excuse me" when you sneeze. Don't hold your hands over your head to speak; stand straight; now talk.

—*Odette Clayton Charbonnet, Joyce Charbonnet Hayward's mother*

Young ladies never
call boys.

—*A friend's mother*

God don't like ugly.

—*Annette Madden's mother*

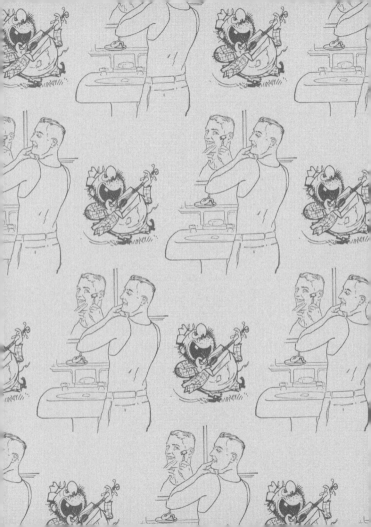

2

Men:
Can't Live with 'Em and Can't Live without 'Em

Love them or hate them? Mothers can't
make up their minds. What is true is that
they want their daughters to have happy
relationships; just how to achieve that
is open for speculation.

A piece of man is better
than no man at all.

—*A mom*

*N*o man is better than
a piece of a man.

—*Cynthia Harris, Alisa's mother*

*A*ny woman can marry if she sets her standards low enough.

—*Deidre Marion Charlot, Myra Hayward Marion's mother*

*D*on't need a man, but let him believe that you do.

—*Judy Craig, Nara Brados's mother*

[**W**]omen are simply going to have to take over this world and that's all there is to it. All men want to do is start wars and show off in front of each other . . . most of them don't get past age twelve.

—*Mother, in* Standing in the Rainbow

*W*hatever women do they must do twice as well as men to be thought half as good. Luckily, this is not difficult.

—*Charlotte Whitton*

*N*ever a foot so crooked as a shoe won't fit it.

—*A friend's mother*

40

*T*hese same men who run around with their heads laid back and their tongues hanging out . . . don't worry—Father Time will take care of all that.

—*Lucinda Smith, Gwendolyn Goodbeer's mother*

*W*omen prefer men who
have something tender
about them—especially
the legal kind.

—*Kay Graham*

*M*en are like streetcars:
there's always one coming
down the track.

—*Robin Mastro's mother*

***N*ever** say "I told you so"
to your husband, even when
you told him so.

—Liza Gutierrez-O'Neill's mother

***N*ever** marry a man that
looks better than you.

—A friend's mother

Why buy the cow when the milk's for free?

—*Robin Mastro's mom*

*N*ever swim with boys.
Sperm floats.

—*Naomi Judd, Ashley and*
Wynonna's mother

*M*en are the tears of God.

—*Egyptian mothers*

*D*on't start anything that you can't keep up (especially when it comes to doing something for men).

—*Cheryl Z. Moore's mother*

*G*ood riddance to
bad rubbish.

—*A friend's mother, regarding
her daughter's break-up*

*M*arry a man younger than
you and he will always keep you
young at heart.

—*A mom*

*W*hat's good for the
goose is good for
the gander.

—*Marlene Charbonnet's mother*

*M*arry someone rich so
that you can support your
parents in their old age.

—*Necia Velenchenko's mother*

*N*ever trust a man.

—*My mother*

*T*he secret to a successful marriage is to marry a man who loves you a bit more than you love him.

—*A friend's mother*

*B*ring a hatpin with you, dear, just in case your date gets fresh.

—*Robin Mastro's mom*

*D*on't marry the guy. Live with him first so you can get to know him.

—*Yolanda Asher's mother*

*W*omen are cursed, and men are the proof.

—*Rosanne Barr*

*Y*ou judge a man by how he does walk. If he walk brisk or slapdash or to show himself off, or day-dreamy or idle— the walk will betray him.

—*Mother, in* The Ventriloquist's Tale

*N*ever trust a man that
doesn't wear socks with
his dress shoes.

—*Iren Luciano*

*N*o matter how in love you are with someone, if you've lost sight of who you are and you're loving yourself a little less, it's time to walk away.

—*Emily Sauber's mom*

Men are pigs.

—Yolanda Asher's mother

Don't count on a man to buy you the finer things in life— buy them for yourself.

—A friend's mother

*S*ex is not good.

—*Queen Latifa's mom*

*A*lways have a man
as a roommate because
you'll be safer.

—*Susan Asbjornson's mother*

*N*o matter how much
success you find, nothing
compares to the love of a man.

—*My mother*

*N*o man is perfect.

—*A friend's mother, when she got cold feet
before her wedding*

57

*I*f you meet a man who can wait until after marriage to have sex, ditch him quick. His libido is too low to satisfy anyone in this family.

—*Marilyn Webber's mom*

*T*he secret to a long marriage is separate bathrooms.

—*Nancy King's mother*

*I*t doesn't matter if you are not really attracted to him, because once you get married, you won't have much sex anymore anyway!

—*A friend's mother, on "a good catch"*

*D*on't ever sit
on a boy's lap.

—*Sarah Quigley's mother*

*D*on't depend on any man to
take care of you.

—*Yolanda Asher's mother*

*D*on't get married. Don't rush yourself. Live life.

—*Oracene Price, Venus and Serena Williams's mother*

*A*ll boys know when you are having your period . . . they are like wild dogs.

—*Robin Mastro's mom*

*T*here are forty men in the world who are right for you.

—*Nancy King's mother*

*I*f you want something said, ask a man; if you want something done, ask a woman.

—*Margaret Thatcher*

*Y*ou can't control
who you love.

—*A friend's mother*

*F*rench kissing is
a mortal sin.

—*Cheryl Murphy Durzy's mother*

*M*en are just like gardens.
You have to tend to them
every day or they just
go to seed.

—*Mother, in* Standing in the Rainbow

$\mathcal{I}$f you have a choice between marrying two men, always marry the man whose name is closest to the beginning of the alphabet. Everything in life goes in alphabetical order.

—*Marilyn Webber's mom*

*I*f you get married, make
sure you keep a separate
account of your own money
as a safety net.

—*Yolanda Asher's mother*

*I*t's just as easy to marry a
rich man as it is a poor one.

—*Robin Mastro's mom (and several others!)*

3

Succeeding on Life's Highways and Byways

In the quest for the best for their children, mothers dole out many notions about how to make it in the world. Each one has her own ideas—you decide which gems to keep.

*J*ust try your best.

—*My mother*

*Y*our best friend is the
dollar in your pocket.

—*George Lopez's mom*

*D*on't worry about things over which you have no control.

—*Goldie W. Chavenson,*
Deborah Grossman's mother

*Y*ou're going to be glad you did [take a risk]. It's good for you.

—*A friend's mom, when*
whatever she was doing
didn't feel good

*J*ust keep living!

—*Nancy Thompson's mother*

*H*appiness is *not* the
goal of life.

—*Dotty Cala's mother*

Know when to hold 'em and when to fold 'em.

—Ruby Jean Roberson,
Marsha Lang-Collins's mother

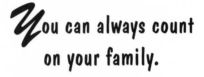

*Y*ou can always count
on your family.

—*Gaynelle Henger's mom*

*T*he only person you can
count on is yourself.

—*My mother*

*W*hat doesn't kill you
makes you stronger.

—*A friend's mother*

*I*f I put it on your
back, someone can take
it away from you. If I
put it in your head,
no one can.

—*Elsie McGuire, Marne Benedict's mother*

Do unto others before they do unto you.

—Odette Clayton Charbonnet, Joyce Charbonnet Hayward's mother

Make sure to get that piece of paper in order to prepare yourself for life.

—Rae Louise Hayward, referring to a college degree

Nothing beats a failure but a try.

—*Ruth Manuel-Logan's mother*

Ask Jesus.

—*Mother, in* In the Name of Salome

77

*N*ever be afraid of hard work. Hard work never hurt anyone. Work is good for you.

—*Gaynelle Henger's mom*

*D*on't write no check that
your mouth can't cash.

—*A friend's mother*

*L*et your "yes" mean yes,
and your "no" mean no.

—*John Moore's mother*

*N*ever hold back a question. You will get further ahead when you do [ask], you'll be at the same point if you don't.

—*Shari Ilalaole's mother*

*T*hink about the consequences before you take the action.

—*Judy Craig, Nara Brados's mother*

The world isn't fair. The sooner you figure that out, the less heartache you'll have.

—*Mama Clark, mother of seven*

If it ain't broke, don't fix it.

—*A friend's mother*

Nobody said life was fair.

—Goldie W. Chavenson,
Deborah Grossman's mother

You have nothing to lose by asking.

—Mother Earnestine, to her nine
children, including Tomyē

*I*t's okay to cry and get it all out—for fifteen to twenty minutes max; then get up and get busy!

—*Ann Marie, Reba's mother*

*I*f you don't want to become a professional liar, don't practice telling lies.

—*Cheryl Z. Moore's mother*

*T*he only way to succeed is
to go to college.

—*Will Smith's mother*

*D*uty is the highest virtue.

—*Mother, in* In the Name of Salome

***U*nderstand the difference between what you want to do and what must be done.**

—*John Moore's mother*

***W*omen must learn to be independent.**

—*A friend's mother*

*Y*ou need to learn
to be patient.

—*Gaynelle Henger's mother*

*I*f you think too much, you
miss all the steps.

—*Mothers from the Bayou*

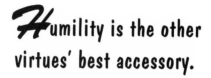

*H*umility is the other virtues' best accessory.

—*Naomi Judd, Ashley and Wynonna's mother*

*I*f the ice is thin, one must walk fast.

—*Russian mothers*

Keep your expectations
low because you'll never
be disappointed.

—*Goldie W. Chavenson,*
Deborah Grossman's mother

You'll have to learn
to stop crying or you'll
never get anywhere.

—*Mother Earnestine, to her nine*
children, including Tomyē

*I*f you want it to change,
do something about it.

—*Gaynelle Henger's mom*

*I*t's bad luck to begin
work on Fridays.

—*Southern mothers*

89

*I*f you act as good as you
look, you'll be fine.

—*Ame Beanland's mother*

*I*f you keep doing what you've
done, you'll keep getting
what you've got.

—*A friend's mother*

*W*hatever situation you
find yourself in, think of what
the Virgin Mary would do
and do the same.

—*Irish mothers*

*A*lways spend more money on books than on beauty products.

—*Emily Sauber's mom*

*N*o matter what *you* say or
do, people are always gonna do
what *they* wanna do!

—*Elayne Howard's mother*

*T*omorrow will be
better than today.

—*A friend's mom*

93

4

Playing Nicely with Others

For most of us, despite the gender revolution, Mom was the one who was concerned with our getting along well with other people. In today's terminology, she taught us emotional intelligence.

*I*t's important to treat everyone you meet with respect, because you never know who you may have to ask for a glass of water.

—*Landon's mom*

*D*on't hit on the head.

—*My mother,*
while swatting me on the head

*N*ever tell anyone anything
that you don't want told.

—*A friend's mother*

*Y*our back won't break
if you bend it.

—*Egyptian mothers*

*D*on't draw attention
to yourself.

—Irish mothers

*W*hen you go to someone's
house [and] they give you
something, say "thank you."

—Odette Clayton Charbonnet, Joyce
Charbonnet Hayward's mother

*B*e nice to your sister.
It's good for you.

—Gaynelle Henger's mother

*I*f someone is mean to you,
compliment them.

—Susan Asbjornson's mother

*A*lways say "thank you"
and "please."

—*Shari Ilalaoe's mother*

*T*hose who turn a deaf ear
respond with clichés.

—*Armaveni Kazarian-Hamparian,*
Lucine's grandmother

***D**on't go around hitting other people's children.*

—Elayne Howard's mother

***B**low your nose and say hi to this lady.*

—Sylvie Galiana's mother

*Y*ou can only be phony for so long. Always be yourself.

—*Delores Madison's mother*

*N*o one can use you unless you allow it!

—*Deborah Vaughan's mother*

*H*e who angers you,
conquers you.

—*Elizabeth Kenney's mom*

*W*hen you are in school,
your teacher is just like your
parents, so make sure you
listen and be good.

—*Joyce Hayward,*
Rae Louise Hayward's mother

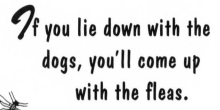

*I*f you lie down with the
dogs, you'll come up
with the fleas.

—*A friend's mother*

*N*ever get involved with
someone who is more messed
up in the head than you are.

—*John Moore's mother*

I want everyone to like you, so you will wear a party dress and high heels, even though your friends are all going in jeans.

—*Mary Margaret Carlisle's mother*

*F*ind out what the kids want and give it to them. Finding out what they want is the hard part.

—*Goldie W. Chavenson,*
Deborah Grossman's mother

*T*hey're just jealous of you.

—*Yolanda Asher's mother, when other kids*
were mean to her

*T*he mosquito wastes his time when he tries to sting the alligator.

—*Mothers from the Bayou*

*W*hat will other
people think?

—*Jan Powell's mother*

*D*on't say you don't like
eggs or your sister
will start hating
them too.

—*M.J. Ryan's mother*

*R*emember: people talk "stink" about others because *they* have little self-esteem. Rise above that.

—*Shari Ilalaole's mother*

*Y*ou can't change people's nature. You can't say to a bird, "Be more like a cow."

—*Mother, in* Standing in the Rainbow

Never say you're sorry unless you mean it.

—*Emily Sauber's mom*

Don't talk back.

—*Jan Powell's mother*

*W*hat children know, they learn inside the home—they don't lick it off the sidewalk.

—*Goldie W. Chavenson,*
Deborah Grossman's mother

*Y*ou can catch a lot more flies with honey than you can with vinegar.

—*A friend's mother*

111

*D*on't get a swelled head.

—*Irish mothers*

*T*reat others the way you
want to be treated.

—*Shari Ilalaole's mother*

If you can't laugh, you can't keep a good friend.

—*Mothers from the Bayou*

It's good to be smart, but it's better to get along.

—*Helen Lindgren, to her daughter Karen Bradford in* Real Simple *magazine*

*L*eave that mean woman.
If she's mean to you now,
she'll be mean to you later.

—*Orleans Hopkins,*
to her son Steven Hopkins

I do what I do. You can
take it or leave it.

—*Goldie W. Chavenson,*
Deborah Grossman's mother

*D*on't be coming out
with all that.

—*Irish mothers*

*I*f you keep your mouth shut,
you won't catch flies.

—*Mothers from the Bayou*

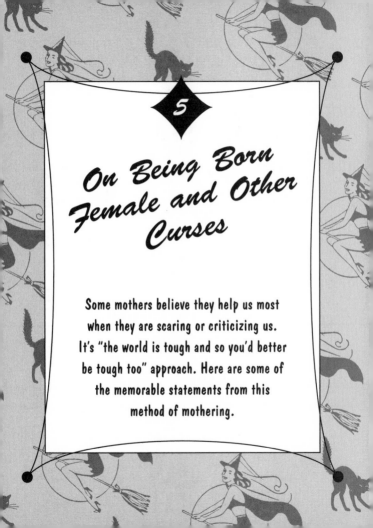

5

On Being Born Female and Other Curses

Some mothers believe they help us most when they are scaring or criticizing us. It's "the world is tough and so you'd better be tough too" approach. Here are some of the memorable statements from this method of mothering.

*R*aising a daughter is like watering your neighbor's lawn.

—*Chinese mothers*

*B*eauty is the first present nature gives to women and the first it takes away.

—*Anonymous mother*

*E*ven cheap tea tastes
good on the first brewing.
Even a witch's daughter is
beautiful at eighteen.

—*Japanese mother, in Takashi
Matsuoka's* Cloud of Sparrows

*W*hen you leave home and get rich, you can lie on the psychiatrist's couch and tell them what a b**** I was. In the meantime, just do what I say.

—*Goldie W. Chavenson,*
Deborah Grossman's mother

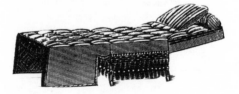

*T*hink good thoughts when you are pregnant. Mothers can poison their babies with bad thoughts.

—*Latin American mothers*

*D*on't put new shoes on the table. You will bring us bad luck.

—*A friend's mother*

121

*Y*ou can never be too thin or too rich.

—*Christine Filippone's mother*

*I*f you don't behave, I'll get your good eye.

—*Lois Lay Castiglioni's
North Georgia mother*

*I*f you hit your mother, your arm will stay like that [in a hitting position] when you are put into your casket.

—*Odette Clayton Charbonnet, Joyce Charbonnet Hayward's mother*

*D*on't walk away from me
when I'm talking to you.
Now get out of here!

—*Bethany Schwartz's mother*

A hard head makes
for a sore behind.

—*Ginette Crout Baker,
Alisha Johnson's mother*

You're so stupid, you would
not find water in a lake.

—*Sylvie Galiana's mother*

Go play on the freeway.

—*Nancy Girard, Eric Girard's mother, to
Eric and his siblings when they were noisy*

*I*f a girl isn't beautiful at fifteen, she never will be.

—*A friend's mother*

A woman should obey her father in youth, her husband in maturity, and her son in old age.

—*Chinese mothers*

126

*W*hen you'll come to age
and have all your vaccinations,
then you will be able to
decide by yourself.

—*Sylvie Galiana's mother*

*T*hink about the starving
children in China.

—*Bessie Sasek, Kay Sasek's mother*

I just know you're going to marry a rich man, so by God, you're going to do your share of housework now.

—*A friend's mother,*
when her daughter was six

You'll give your father a heart attack.

—My mother, whenever I was doing something she disapproved of.

*D*on't let a black cat cross
your path or you'll
have bad luck.

—*Southern mothers*

*Y*ou must have self-control.

—*Jan Powell's mother*

*N*obody likes a clown.

—*Nancy Girard, Eric Girard's mother, when he was trying to be class clown all the time*

*S*omeday you're going to have a child just like you.

—*A friend's mother, when she was misbehaving*

131

*Y*our dad loves you even though it does not feel like it.

—*Gaynelle Henger's mother*

*I*f you sleep in the car, it will drive away in the middle of the night . . . and we won't be able to find you.

—*Cheryl Murphy Durzy's mother*

*E*at that liver! Don't you realize that a baby died to feed you?

—*Mary Margaret Carlisle's mother*

*I*f you loved me, you wouldn't disagree with me.

—*Sarah Quigley's mother*

*I*f you are a woman,
growing old is hell.

—*A friend's mother,
when she was forty*

*S*ingle mothers can't
be one of the boys.

—*Mother, in* Mapping the Edge

*O*f course you don't
feel that way.

—*Jan Powell's mother*

I'm just going to let
you stew in your own
juices for awhile.

—*My mother, when I was upset*

*Y*ou are so coldhearted
you might as well
have vinegar in your veins.

—*A friend's mother, when she wouldn't
do what her mother wanted*

I taught you to be
independent, but I made
you too independent.

—*My mother, while lamenting that I didn't
listen enough to her advice*

136

Eat a grapefruit.

—Barb Parmet's mother, every time
she reached for a cookie

You're becoming the man
you wanted to marry.

—A friend's mother

*W*hen you're sick, you shouldn't look in the mirror or else your soul might fly into the glass and you'll die.

—*Mothers in Victorian England*

138

*A*nswer me! Don't talk with
food in your mouth!

—*Erma Bombeck's mother*

*D*on't let anyone in
the family know.

—*Jan Powell's mother*

*I*s your eye falling out?
If not, you're okay.

—A friend's mother

*Y*ou look like
something dragged
through a hedge
backward.

—Mother, in Grace Notes

If you don't stop crying, you are going to cry your eyes out of your head.

—*Mothers in Victorian England*

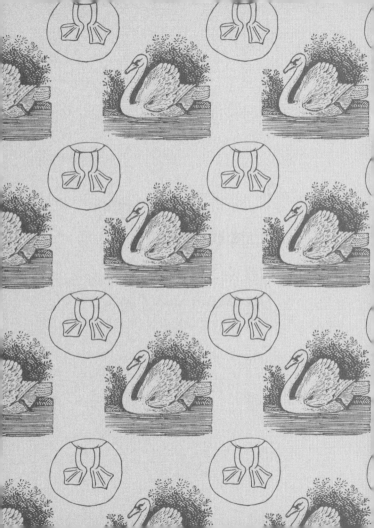

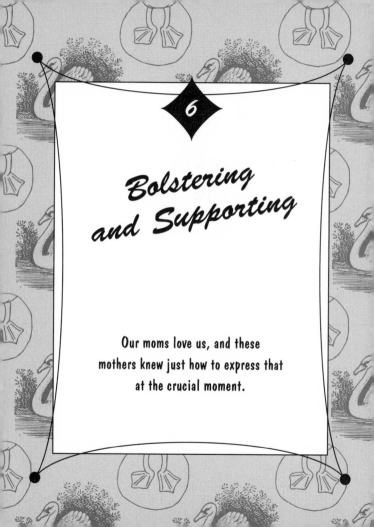

6

Bolstering and Supporting

Our moms love us, and these
mothers knew just how to express that
at the crucial moment.

*W*hatever you do and any way the wind blows, you're all right with me.

—*Ann Marie, Reba's mother*

*L*ove with all of your heart.

—*Susan Marjorie Tuttle Martin, Jennifer's mother*

Big feet and small ankles are a sign of grace and beauty.

—*Christine Filippone's mother,
who wore a size ten*

*Y*ou're just as good
as—or better than—
anyone on the radio. You
need to keep going.

—LL Cool J's mother, in
In Style *magazine*

146

*Y*ou can do anything you
want if you set your
mind to it.

—*Naomi Judd's mother*

*T*ell your children every
day how much you love
them—and why.

—*M.J. Ryan, Ana Li's mother*

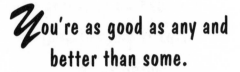

*Y*ou're as good as any and
better than some.

—*Marian Press Yap's friend's mother*

*B*ut I've always thought you
were so beautiful!

—*A friend's mother, when she told her how
ugly she thought she was*

$\mathcal{Y}$ou have a good head on
your shoulders, and I know
you will always make
the right choices.

—*Susan Pugliese's mother*

*T*he reason the food is so good is that I put lots of love in the pots as I cook.

—*Lucinda Smith,*
Gwendolyn Goodbeer's mother

I love you most.

—*A friend's grandmother, to all
her grandkids*

*Y*ou are not fat. You have a
great body. You are the
most beautiful girl in
the whole world.

—*Susan Asbjornson's mother*

151

***D*on't worry. The ugly duckling always grows into the beautiful swan.**

—*Ruth Segall, Judith Segall's mother*

***Y*ou are a great comfort to me.**

—*A friend's mom*

*W*hen in doubt, listen to
what your intuition says.

—*Susan Marjorie Tuttle Martin,
to her daughter Jennifer*

*T*here are many
fish in the sea.

—*Ruth Segall, Judith Segall's mother, when
Judith was recovering from a break-up*

7

*Keeping
the Home Fires
Burning*

Moms have so much to say about
creating a well-run household—and we
were listening!

*E*very woman needs
her own house.

—*Ann Marie, Reba's mother*

*T*he wife who runs her
house well is a treasure
beyond price.

—*Egyptian mother, in* The Wise Woman

*A*lways pick up
after yourself.

—*Daphne Rose Kingma's mother*

157

*C*leanliness is next
to godliness.

—*Elayne Howard's mother*

*M*ake your bed every
morning and you'll never
want for a husband.

—*A friend's mother*

*D*on't throw away dirty
water until you have clean.

—*Toinette Lippe*

*T*ake your shoes off
in the house.

—*Nancy Girard, Eric Girard's mother*

*T*he best time to clean
house is Saturday morning—
everyone should help.

—*Gaynelle Henger's mom*

*U*se a little elbow grease!

—*My mother, when I failed to
clean something properly*

*T*he truth of a house
is its cleanliness.

—*Mother, in* Paneb

*S*nip off dead blossoms and
a plant will flower more.

—*Connie Spencer's mother*

I dreamed of fish last night.
We are going to have
good luck today.

—*Odette Clayton Charbonnet, Joyce
Charbonnet Hayward's mother*

*T*o cure an earache,
stew some earthworms
and use the fat.

—*Southern mothers*

*D*o the laundry on Monday, ironing on Tuesday, grocery shopping on Friday, and housecleaning on Saturday when the kids are around to help.

—*My mother*

*A*lways keep a bottle of brandy in a cupboard in case someone is taken ill suddenly.

—*My mother*

*N*ever let a cat into a house when you have a baby. It will suck the baby's breath away.

—*Irish mothers*

A maid does not do it right.

—*Gaynelle Henger's mother*

*B*reaking a mirror is
seven years bad luck.

—*A friend's mother*

*D*on't step
over a broom or you'll
have bad luck. To reverse the
luck, step over it backwards.

—*Southern mothers*

*D*on't open that umbrella in the house! That's bad luck.

—*A friend's mother*

*T*o get soft hair, collect rainwater in a barrel and use it for rinsing.

—*My mother*

*D*on't put it down.
Put it away.

—*Susan Marjorie Tuttle Martin,*
to her daughter Jennifer

I'll cook like that when
I have a sous-chef
and a dishwasher.

—*Goldie W. Chavenson, Deborah Grossman's*
mother, watching a TV chef

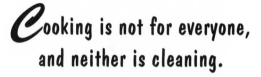

Cooking is not for everyone,
and neither is cleaning.

—*Deborah, Naomi Wolf's mother, in*
Real Simple *magazine*

Never kiss a cat. It is
full of germs.

—*Irish mothers*

169

7he bread you bake by your own sweat tastes better than the dishes of sultans.

—*Armenian mothers*

There are three different kinds of clean: boat-clean, camp-clean, and house-clean. Be sure you know what's what.

—*Susan Marjorie Tuttle Martin,*
to daughter Jennifer

*T*hrow out the margarine.
Feed me butter.

—*Goldie W. Chavenson, Deborah
Grossman's mother*

*N*o wet towels on the bed.

—*Edith Mary Wheeldon Martin,
to her children and grandchildren*

*C*lose the door—we don't live in a barn.

—*My mother*

*I*f the seam is not straight, rip it out.

—*Gaynelle Henger's mom*

*C*lean off your dinner plate
so that your betrothed's
complexion will be clear.

—*Lusia Der Kasbarian, quoting an
Armenian proverb*

*D*irt won't kill you unless it falls down on top of you.

—*Catherine Palmer, Opal Palmer Adisa's mother*

*I*f you spill the salt, throw some over your left shoulder.

—*A friend's mother*

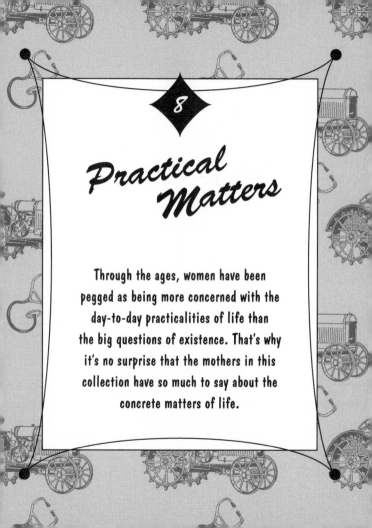

8

Practical Matters

Through the ages, women have been pegged as being more concerned with the day-to-day practicalities of life than the big questions of existence. That's why it's no surprise that the mothers in this collection have so much to say about the concrete matters of life.

*Y*ou can always teach.

—*Molly Fumia's mother,*
on a fall-back profession for women

*W*atch out for
tiggers and flies.

—*A friend's mother*

Don't throw good money after bad.

—*Emelene Heim, Donna Heim's mother*

What have we got to be ashamed of? It's good, clean dirt.

—Susan Geer's mom, after working all day re-roofing the house, stripping wallpaper, mixing cement, planting, or doing any of the hundreds of other things a single mom does herself with the kid helping in order to make ends meet.

*A*lways carry at least three dollars in your wallet.

—*Ami DeAvilla's mom*

*L*ove doesn't pay for the (rent, utilities, groceries), and even if it did, most of us know our love check would bounce.

—*Delores Madison's mother*

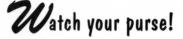

*W*atch your purse!

—*Gail E. Cantor's mom*

*D*o not overload yourself
with bills or babies.

—*A friend's mother*

Give me my flowers while I can smell them.

—*Odette Clayton Charbonnet, Joyce Charbonnet Hayward's mother*

You have to get up real early in the morning to pull the wool over my eyes!

—*Elayne Howard's mother*

*F*unk and fume don't mix.
[In other words, if you
stink, don't cover it
with perfume.]

—*La Sandra Ivy's mother*

*I*f a cut itches,
it means it is healing.

—*My mother*

*U*se toilet paper to cover
the toilet seat in a public
restroom because you could get
some kind of infection.

—*Robyn Greene's mother*

*I*f it's too good to be
true, then it really is.

—*Anita M. Dyer, Anika R. Dyer's mother*

*E*at whole wheat and grains.
Don't use hairspray.
Protect yourself
from the sun.

—*Marian Howell Price Tuttle,
to her daughter Susan Marjorie
Tuttle Martin*

*B*usiness is business!

—*A friend's mother*

I need that useless
thing like a third tit.

—*Goldie W. Chavenson,*
Deborah Grossman's mother

N ever let your left hand
know what your right
hand is doing.

—*Odette Clayton Charbonnet, Joyce*
Charbonnet Hayward's mother

187

*N*ever sit on a public toilet. Squat over it.

—*My mother*

*G*o on out in the rain, darlin'—you're not made of sugar so you won't melt!

—*A friend's mother*

Don't tell the tax collectors
everything you know.

—*Sarah Quigley's mother*

Don't get
caught
speeding.

—*Susan Marjorie Tuttle Martin,*
to her daughter Jennifer

Don't put beans
in your ears.

—*My mother*

If that isn't the real thing,
there ain't a cow in Texas.

—*Odette Clayton Charbonnet, Joyce
Charbonnet Hayward's mother*

*W*ash your hands when
you come in from outside.
Who knows what germs
you picked up?

—*Nancy Girard, Eric Girard's mother*

*T*alking about pumpkins
doesn't make them grow.

—*Mother, in*
The No. 1 Ladies' Detective Agency

*Y*ou must have a *knippel* [literally a "pinch" or "piece" of something]. Steal a dollar from the grocery money and put it away.

—*Goldie W. Chavenson's mother*

*D*on't shoot the horse until you pay for the tractor.

—*A friend's mother*

*T*o keep cut flowers fresh
longer, add an aspirin
to the water.

—*My mother*

*S*tay out of the pool for
thirty minutes after eating.

—*Lori Pottinger's mother*

193

Drink eight glasses of water every day.

—Marian Howell Price Tuttle to her daughter Susan Marjorie Tuttle Martin

Potato skins are poisonous.

—Christine Filippone's mother, who ate everyone's skins after they left the table.

*N*ot every skinned
teeth is laughter.

—*Catherine Palmer, Opal Palmer*
Adisa's mother

*Y*ou'll have good news if a
buzzard flies over your house.

—*Southern mothers*

*Y*ou get what you pay for.

—*A friend's mother*

*F*ind something else to do so
the time will go faster.
[a.k.a. Think about
something nice and the time
will go faster.]

—*My mother, said as a way of dealing with
the dentist drilling without Novocain.*

*B*e grateful we are not the
Whittenburgs.

—*Gaynelle Henger's mom*

*D*on't forget your coat!

—*Andrea Hurst's mom*

197

Better out than in!

—A friend's mother, when they passed gas or belched

*N*o one wants to eat at
a restaurant with no
cars parked outside.

—*Marcie Montgomery's mother*

*D*rink a glass of warm
milk if you can't sleep.

—*A friend's mother*

*Employment is
nature's physician.*

—*Mother, in*
Behind the Scenes at the Museum

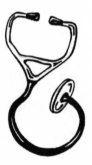

*D*on't forget to bang
the mailbox handle four or
five times to be *sure*
the letter goes down.

—*Anne Hollingworth's mother*

*D*on't complain.
When I was young, I had to
drink cod liver oil.

—*My mother,*
whenever we complained
about some food we
didn't like

Cutting off a mule's ears won't make him a horse.

—*Mothers from the Bayou*

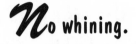

*N*o whining.

—*Gaynelle Henger's mom*

*T*o bring on rain,
hang a snake on a fence.

—*Southern mothers*

***W**arm weather colds are the worst.*

—My mother

***D**on't eat that. It'll shoot your eye out.*

—Brendan Fraser's mom, when she wanted to keep him from eating something

*L*earn to type and take
shorthand—you'll
always have a job.

—*Gaynelle Henger's mother.*

*D*on't go out with wet hair.

—*Andrea Hurst's mom*

For a great shine, rinse your hair in vinegar or beer.

—My mother, who apparently didn't mind smelling like a salad or a brewery, when caught in a rainstorm

Don't tell me how the cow ate the cabbage!

—Cynthia Cotton, Blythe Cotton's mother

I t's closed for painting.

—Sharon Osbourne, when her
kids wanted her to go somewhere.

T he sea air is good for you.

—My mother

*L*ie down and eat
some saltines.

*—Kay Snyder's cure for whatever
ails you, in* In Style *magazine*

I'm cold. Go put
on a sweater.

—A friend's mother

*W*hen you need a parking place, go directly to where you want to be and you'll find a space.

—*Goldie W. Chavenson,*
Deborah Grossman's mother

*I*f I'm lying, I'm crying.

—*Odette Clayton Charbonnet, Joyce*
Charbonnet Hayward's mother

*A*nything worth doing
is worth doing well.

*—Rex Browning's mom, whenever
Rex wasn't doing something well*

*E*at your soup and you
will get tall.

—Sylvie Galiana's mother

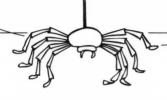

*I*f you find a spider on your
coat, you'll have good luck.

—*Southern mothers*

*T*oo many cooks
spoil the broth.

—*Alice Simms, Annette Madden's mother*

If a ladybug lands on you, [and] if you make a wish before it flies away, your wish will come true.

—*My mother*

213

*Y*ou know you need new glasses when you can't see the score on the football screen of the TV.

—*Goldie W. Chavenson,*
Deborah Grossman's mother

*S*implicity!
Simplicity! Simplicity!

—*92-year-old Marian Howell Price Tuttle,*
to her daughter Susan Marjorie Tuttle
Martin, when planning her memorial service

*A*s the monkey said when he caught his tail in the door: It won't be long now!

—*Synolve Flakes Moore, Iris Moore's*
mother, whenever Iris asked how much longer

*I*f you can't stand the heat, get out of the kitchen.

—Alice Simms, Annette Madden's mother

I'm tired. It's time
for your nap.

—*A friend's mother*

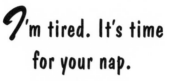

*E*at your carrots.
They make you
kind.

—*Sylvie Galiana's mother*

Never put soap on your face. It dries it out.

—*My mother*

*I*f Mama ain't happy, nobody's happy.

—*Many mothers*

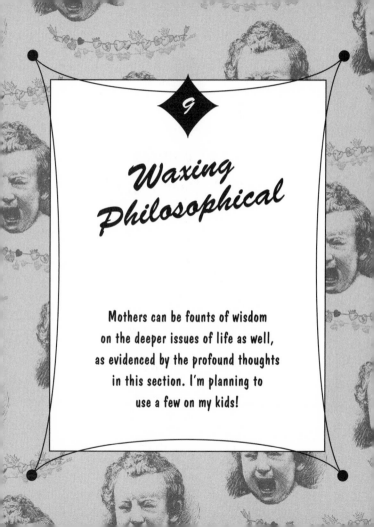

9

Waxing Philosophical

Mothers can be founts of wisdom
on the deeper issues of life as well,
as evidenced by the profound thoughts
in this section. I'm planning to
use a few on my kids!

*D*on't play in the same
pasture that you graze in.

—*Ruth Segall, Judith Segall's mother*

*I*f you can't change
your situation, change
your attitude.

—*Suvan Geer's mom*

*T*he wildflower on the
mountaintop will not
trade places with the
rose in the garden.

—*Armenian mothers*

I can live in hell three days
if I know I'm getting out.

—*Sandra Varner's mother*

*D*on't worry, baby. Leave it
in God's hands. Be still.

—*Lucinda Smith, Gwendolyn
Goodbeer's mother*

*C*ount your blessings
before they happen.

—*Odette Clayton Charbonnet, Joyce
Charbonnet Hayward's mother*

*A*fter you have swallowed
the donkey, don't
choke on the tail.

—*Helen Katsufrakis's*
mother-in-law

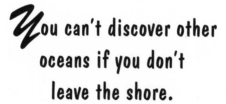

*Y*ou can't discover other
oceans if you don't
leave the shore.

—*John Moore's mother*

*B*eauty is only skin deep,
but ugly is to the bones.
When beauty has gone,
ugly lingers on.

—*A friend's mother*

*I*f you make your bed hard,
you'll have to turn over often.

—*Cheryl Z. Moore's mother*

The wheel that squeaks gets the oil.

—A friend's mother

*I*t's not what you gather, but what you scatter that tells what kind of life you've lived.

—*Cynthia Carr's mom*

*F*reedom is a blessing.

—*Oracene Price, Serena and Venus Williams's mother*

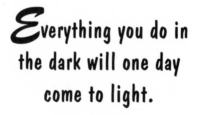

*E*verything you do in
the dark will one day
come to light.

—*Tina Knowles,*
Beyonce Knowles's mother

*T*hink of your life like a sack of beans, daughter. There are only so many. . . . If you eat too many all at once, you can live for years with nothing to show for it but gas.

—*Mother,* in The Fruit of Stone

*L*ittle ones pull at your
apron strings, but older ones
pull at your heart strings.

—*Nida Shoecraft Anderson McKnight*

*H*oney, it's gotta get better because it can't get any worse than this.

—*Lori Pottinger's mother*

*I*f I had to choose between book sense and common sense in someone, I'll choose common sense.

—*Patricia Ashton's mother*

*T*here is a right way to do everything. There's even a right way to do the wrong thing.

—*Anna Crout Jones, Bob Jones' mother*

*R*emember: tigers never change their stripes!

—*Anne Hollingworth's mother*

When faced with a
room full of horse s***,
look for the horse.

—*Susan, Jennifer Bernal
Martin Brown's mother*

From your mouth
to God's ears.

—*Goldie W. Chavenson, Deborah Grossman's
mother, whenever someone says something
positive about the future*

It's terrible not to be able
to hear, but it's worse
not being able to listen.
There's a difference.

—*Mother*, *in* Grace Notes

*O*uter beauty means nothing because it fades.

—*Tina Knowles, Beyonce Knowles's mother*

*S*o goes life in a pickle factory.

—*Adrienne D. Herman's grandmother, when things were tough*

*G*od works in
mysterious ways.

—*Cathy DeForest's mother*

*C*rying over it won't make
it clean. Life moves on and
you have to move with it.

—*Mother, in* Hope Floats

237

*W*hen the herd reversed
direction, the lame
became the leaders.

—*Armenian mothers*

*I*t's not the cards you're
dealt, it's the way
that you play them.

—*Mother, in* Mapping the Edge

238

*T*here's nothing slower
than a wet week.

—*Australian mothers*

*T*he world will
pinch you if
you let it, so
don't let it.

—*Mother,* *in* The Passion
of Artemisia

*N*either a scrooge
nor a patsy be.

—Suvan Geer's mother

A wise man changes,
but a fool never does.

—Ruby Jean Roberson,
Marsha Lang-Collins's mother

240

*E*verything that happens—
every treat, every adventure,
every mishap or triumph—is
an investment in your memory
bank. It will pay dividends
later. Nothing is wasted.

—*Mother, in* Flight

*E*veryone has skeletons in their closet.

—*My mother, when I was feeling sorry for myself*

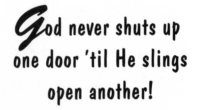

*G*od never shuts up one door 'til He slings open another!

—*Mother, in* Standing in the Rainbow

*W*hen you're feeling sorry
for yourself, remember
that others are worse
off and brighten up.

—*A friend's mother*

*F*ollow the light.

—*Mother, in* In the Name of Salome

*B*eauty isn't something to be proud of because you didn't earn it. It just happened. Intelligence is something to be proud of because you worked for it.

—*Emily Sauber's mom*

$\mathcal{L}$ongevity is a good thing.
You get to live a full life.
The bad thing is, you know
you're going to die and
you don't know when.

—*Goldie W. Chavenson,*
Deborah Grossman's mother

*T*hings are never so bad
they can't get worse!

—*Billie McCauley's mother*

*Y*ou can't be brave if
you've only had wonderful
things happen to you.

—*Mary Tyler Moore*

*N*o matter what is happening, keep a positive mental attitude.

—*A friend's mother*

*T*he camel does not see his own hump.

—*Armenian mothers*

*B*e happy now since the
future is uncertain.

—*Italian mothers*

*R*emember what my mother
said, "It will all turn
out for the best."

—*Goldie W. Chavenson,*
Deborah Grossman's mother

***I*f you spit into the wind, it'll hit you in the face.**

—*Kate Hartke's mom*

***O*nly God knows what's next. We put God first in our lives and let Him guide us.**

—*Oracene Price, Venus and Serena Williams's mother*

*L*ife is not one minute,
it is not one hour, it is not
one day. Life is a lifetime.

—*Synolve Flakes Moore,*
Iris Moore's mother

*B*e willing to be willing.

—*Synolve Flakes Moore*
Iris Moore's mother

250

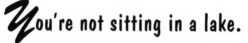 *Y*ou're not sitting in a lake.

—*J. Wallace Swenson's Swedish mother,
whenever Wallace felt impatient*

*A*ll cats are gray at night.

—*Robin Mastro's mom*

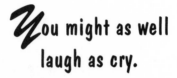

*Y*ou might as well
laugh as cry.

—*Anne Hollingworth's mother*

*N*othing in life is
to be feared. It is
only to be understood.

—*Marie Curie, Irene's mother*

*T*here's always something
to come along to shorten
the tail of the rabbit.

—*Mother, in* Losing Battles

*Y*ou'll go when the
wagon comes for you.

—*Goldie W. Chavenson,*
Deborah Grossman's mother

*L*et a loved one be alive,
though seven mountains away.

—*Armenian mothers*

10

Do They Learn These in Mothers' Training Camp?

Some of what Mama says is universal, ubiquitous. It's as if there is a secret mother school somewhere where they absorb particular sayings before getting pregnant.

*D*on't pick that scab—
it will make it worse.

*N*ever take candy
from strangers.

*D*on't put that in your
mouth. You don't know
where it's been.

Eat up. Children are
starving in (take your pick,
depending on your generation:
China, Russia, Armenia,
Ethiopia . . .)

*G*et a good education.

*W*ait 'til you have
kids of your own!

I don't want to hear
who started it. It takes
two to fight.

*I*f you cross your eyes,
they'll freeze that way.

*D*on't sit too close to the TV or you'll go blind.

*I*f it were a bear it would have bitten you.

*E*at your vegetables.
They're good for you.

*H*urry up!

*D*on't touch.

*S*ay you're sorry.

If you want something
done right,
do it yourself.

*A*lways wear clean underwear. That way if you get hit by a car and end up in the hospital, at least you won't be embarrassed.

*I*f all your friends jump off the bridge, are you going to join them? [a.k.a. If everyone else jumps off the cliff are you going to jump, too?]

*M*en only want one thing.

*Y*ou'll feel better
in the morning.
[a.k.a. Things will look
brighter in the morning.]

*T*here's no such thing
as a free lunch.

*C*ross that bridge
when you come to it.

*I*f you can't say something nice, don't say anything at all.

*N*ever go to bed angry.

*D*on't count your chickens
before they hatch.

*D*on't put all of your
eggs in one basket.

*D*on't bite off more
than you can chew.

*C*hildren should be
seen and not heard.

*A*lways tell the truth.

*S*it up straight.

*D*o as I say, not as I do.

Wait 'til your father gets home!

To Our Readers

Conari Press, an imprint of Red Wheel/Weiser, publishes books on topics ranging from spirituality, personal growth, and relationships to women's issues, parenting, and social issues. Our mission is to publish quality books that will make a difference in people's lives—how we feel about ourselves and how we relate to one another. We value integrity, compassion, and receptivity, both in the books we publish and in the way we do business.

Our readers are our most important resource, and we value your input, suggestions, and ideas about what you would like to see published. Please feel free to contact us, to request our latest book catalog, or to be added to our mailing list.

Conari Press

An imprint of Red Wheel/Weiser, LLC

P.O. Box 612

York Beach, ME 03910-0612

www.conari.com